PRINCEWILL LAGANG

Eco-Entrepreneurs: Building a Green Business Revolution

First published by PRINCEWILL LAGANG 2023

Copyright © 2023 by Princewill Lagang

All rights reserved. No part of this publication may be reproduced, stored or transmitted in any form or by any means, electronic, mechanical, photocopying, recording, scanning, or otherwise without written permission from the publisher. It is illegal to copy this book, post it to a website, or distribute it by any other means without permission.

Princewill Lagang asserts the moral right to be identified as the author of this work.

First edition

This book was professionally typeset on Reedsy. Find out more at reedsy.com

Contents

1. Eco-Entrepreneurs: Building a Green Business Revolution — 1
2. The Roots of Eco-Entrepreneurship — 4
3. The Eco-Entrepreneurs' Playbook — 7
4. The Trailblazers — 11
5. Sectoral Spotlight: Green Innovation Across Industries — 14
6. Regional Resonance: Eco-Entrepreneurship Around the World — 17
7. Nurturing Sustainable Ecosystems — 20
8. Challenges and Resilience — 23
9. Sustainable Success Stories — 26
10. The Future of Eco-Entrepreneurship — 29
11. Taking Action: Becoming an Eco-Entrepreneur — 33
12. A Call to Action — 37

1

Eco-Entrepreneurs: Building a Green Business Revolution

The sun hung low on the horizon, casting a warm, golden hue over the rolling hills and the vast expanse of green that stretched as far as the eye could see. A gentle breeze rustled the leaves of the trees, and the air was filled with the earthy scent of the countryside. This picturesque scene was a stark contrast to the bustling cityscape just a few miles away, where skyscrapers loomed, and the cacophony of modern life was inescapable. It was in this tranquil setting that Sarah Mitchell found her inspiration.

Sarah, a young woman in her early thirties, was a visionary with a passion for the environment. She stood in the midst of a pristine field of wildflowers, her eyes gleaming with determination. With a background in environmental science and a heart that ached for the planet, she had long dreamed of making a difference in the world. But it wasn't until this moment, surrounded by the beauty of nature, that the idea struck her like a lightning bolt: she would become an eco-entrepreneur and set in motion a green business revolution.

This chapter is not just about Sarah; it's about a movement that was quietly gaining momentum in the background, a movement driven by eco-entrepreneurs who were committed to creating businesses that not only thrived but also made the world a better place. These pioneers were challenging the traditional business model, which often prioritized profits over the planet, and they were succeeding in remarkable ways.

The concept of eco-entrepreneurship was rooted in the belief that business could be a force for good. Sarah was not alone in her quest. She was part of a growing tribe of individuals who believed that profitability and sustainability were not mutually exclusive. Their mission was to harness the power of capitalism to drive environmental and social change. And so, with the sun setting behind her, she made a solemn vow to herself and to the world: she would become a trailblazer in this green business revolution.

To understand the genesis of this movement, we must journey back in time to a period when the world was awakening to the stark realities of climate change, resource depletion, and environmental degradation. It was a time of crisis, but it was also a time of opportunity. The global community was coming to terms with the fact that the way we conducted business needed a drastic overhaul, and eco-entrepreneurs emerged as the catalysts of this transformation.

Eco-entrepreneurs were not just dreamers; they were pragmatists who saw the economic potential of green innovation. They were inspired by the triple bottom line – people, planet, and profit. Their businesses were designed to benefit society, reduce their environmental footprint, and make a profit while doing so. The traditional profit-driven approach was evolving into a more holistic and responsible form of capitalism.

In the following chapters, we will delve into the lives and endeavors of these visionary eco-entrepreneurs. Their stories are as diverse as the ecosystems they sought to protect. From renewable energy pioneers in the heart of Silicon Valley to ethical fashion designers in bustling urban centers, these individuals were united by a common purpose – to redefine the role of business in society.

This book will take you on a journey through their successes and challenges, their innovations and aspirations, and their unwavering commitment to building a sustainable future. You will learn how eco-entrepreneurs are not just creating businesses; they are shaping a global movement that transcends borders, industries, and backgrounds.

As the sun dipped below the horizon, Sarah Mitchell's vision became a reality. The green business revolution was afoot, and the stories of eco-entrepreneurs were waiting to be told. Their journey was one of hope, determination, and the belief that by aligning business goals with the well-being of the planet, we could usher in a brighter, greener future for generations to come.

2

The Roots of Eco-Entrepreneurship

The rise of eco-entrepreneurship was not an overnight phenomenon; it had its roots deeply embedded in a growing global consciousness about environmental issues and a pressing need for sustainable solutions. In this chapter, we will explore the historical context and key influencers that set the stage for the green business revolution.

The Environmental Awakening

The 20th century saw significant advancements in technology, industry, and consumerism, leading to unprecedented economic growth and a higher standard of living for many. However, this period of progress came at a great cost to the environment. The exploitation of natural resources, the release of harmful pollutants, and the depletion of ecosystems raised concerns about the long-term viability of such a path.

The 1960s and 1970s marked a turning point when environmental issues began to gain widespread attention. Pioneers like Rachel Carson, with her groundbreaking book "Silent Spring," exposed the devastating impact of pesticides on the environment and ignited the modern environmental movement. Legislation such as the Clean Air Act and the Clean Water Act in the United States signified a growing commitment to regulating and mitigating environmental damage.

The Birth of Corporate Social Responsibility

While environmental concerns were brewing, a parallel shift was happening within the corporate world. The concept of Corporate Social Responsibility (CSR) emerged, suggesting that businesses should take responsibility for their social and environmental impact. Visionary companies began to adopt CSR principles, recognizing that sustainable practices could enhance their brand image and, in some cases, reduce operational costs.

An early pioneer of this mindset was Anita Roddick, the founder of The Body Shop. She built a cosmetics company on the foundation of ethical sourcing, cruelty-free products, and environmental consciousness. Her business demonstrated that profit and ethics were not mutually exclusive. This approach resonated with consumers who were increasingly conscious of the products they purchased and the companies they supported.

The Eco-Entrepreneurial Precursors

Before the term "eco-entrepreneur" became popular, there were trailblazers who set the stage for this emerging movement. People like Amory Lovins, an advocate for energy efficiency and sustainable design, and Muhammad Yunus, who founded Grameen Bank and pioneered microfinance, demonstrated that innovative business models could address social and environmental challenges.

Amory Lovins, in particular, gained recognition for his work at the Rocky Mountain Institute, where he promoted the concept of "natural capitalism." This approach emphasized resource efficiency, renewable energy, and the rethinking of industrial systems. Lovins's ideas inspired a generation of entrepreneurs who would later become champions of green business.

The Eco-Entrepreneur Emerges

By the late 20th century and early 21st century, a new breed of entrepreneurs was emerging – the eco-entrepreneurs. These individuals were not content with superficial greenwashing but were genuinely committed to integrating sustainability into the core of their businesses. They saw environmental challenges as opportunities for innovation and market disruption.

This chapter introduces some of the early eco-entrepreneurs whose stories serve as a blueprint for the green business revolution. From Paul Hawken's book "The Ecology of Commerce" to the founding of Patagonia by Yvon Chouinard, their pioneering efforts exemplify the principles of eco-entrepreneurship. They proved that eco-friendly products and responsible business practices could not only be profitable but also lead to a more sustainable and equitable world.

The eco-entrepreneurial movement was gaining momentum, driven by the confluence of environmental awareness, corporate social responsibility, and the groundbreaking work of its precursors. As the global community grappled with increasingly urgent environmental challenges, these visionary individuals were poised to lead the way toward a greener, more sustainable future.

In the upcoming chapters, we will delve deeper into the stories of eco-entrepreneurs who paved the path for a new era of responsible and sustainable business practices. Their journeys are marked by innovation, resilience, and a passionate commitment to building a better world through entrepreneurship.

3

The Eco-Entrepreneurs' Playbook

The eco-entrepreneurial journey is not a linear one; it's marked by passion, innovation, and a fierce dedication to sustainable principles. In this chapter, we'll explore the strategies, mindset, and key elements that define the playbook of eco-entrepreneurs. Their success is a testament to the fact that building a green business is as much about principles as it is about profits.

1. Visionary Leadership

At the core of every eco-entrepreneur's journey is visionary leadership. These individuals possess a clear and compelling vision for their business and its impact on the environment and society. They are driven by a deep sense of purpose, and this purpose becomes the guiding force behind their decisions and actions.

A prime example of such visionary leadership is the story of Elon Musk, the founder of Tesla. Musk's vision of transitioning the world to sustainable energy through electric vehicles challenged the traditional automotive industry. His unwavering commitment to sustainability and innovation reshaped the electric vehicle landscape and inspired others to follow suit.

2. Innovation and Adaptability

Eco-entrepreneurs thrive on innovation. They are constantly searching for new and creative solutions to environmental challenges. This spirit of innovation is what sets them apart, allowing them to develop groundbreaking products and services that make a positive impact.

One exemplary eco-entrepreneur in this regard is Boyan Slat, the founder of The Ocean Cleanup. Slat's innovative approach to cleaning up plastic waste from the world's oceans involved the deployment of passive plastic collection systems. His groundbreaking technology not only garnered widespread attention but also showcased how innovation can tackle seemingly insurmountable environmental issues.

3. Commitment to Sustainability

Eco-entrepreneurs are unwavering in their commitment to sustainability. They embed eco-conscious practices into every aspect of their business, from sourcing materials and manufacturing processes to supply chain management and waste reduction. This holistic approach ensures that sustainability is not just a marketing buzzword but a fundamental part of their business DNA.

Take the example of Ecover, a company founded by Frans Van Houten and Gunter Pauli. Ecover specializes in eco-friendly cleaning products. From using plant-based ingredients to pioneering phosphate-free detergents, Ecover's commitment to sustainability revolutionized the cleaning product industry.

4. Social Responsibility

Eco-entrepreneurs understand that their responsibilities extend beyond environmental impact. They actively engage in social causes and promote fairness and equality within their organizations. Their businesses become platforms for social change and empowerment.

An inspiring example is the TOMS Shoes model established by Blake Mycoskie. For every pair of shoes sold, TOMS donates a pair to a child in need. Mycoskie's "One for One" model not only transformed the shoe industry but also highlighted the potential of social entrepreneurship to make a difference in the lives of people around the world.

5. Collaboration and Partnerships

Eco-entrepreneurs recognize the power of collaboration. They seek out partnerships with like-minded organizations, nonprofits, and governments to amplify their impact. By working together, they can address larger and more complex environmental and social challenges.

One such collaborative effort is The B Corp Movement, initiated by Jay Coen Gilbert, Bart Houlahan, and Andrew Kassoy. B Corps are for-profit companies certified for meeting rigorous standards of social and environmental performance. The movement has created a community of businesses committed to balancing purpose and profit, encouraging collaboration and collective progress.

6. Resilience and Perseverance

The path of an eco-entrepreneur is often fraught with challenges. Yet, their resilience and unwavering commitment to their mission enable them to overcome obstacles and setbacks. They view failures as opportunities to learn and adapt, ultimately becoming stronger in the process.

The story of Elon Musk's SpaceX exemplifies this resilience. Despite numerous setbacks, including rocket failures and financial struggles, Musk persisted in his goal of reducing space travel costs and making humanity multi-planetary. His tenacity ultimately led to SpaceX's success and the broader goal of human exploration beyond Earth.

The eco-entrepreneurs' playbook is built on these core principles. Their leadership, innovation, commitment to sustainability, social responsibility, collaboration, and resilience are the driving forces behind the green business revolution. In the following chapters, we will dive deeper into the stories of individual eco-entrepreneurs who embody these principles and have achieved remarkable success in their mission to create a more sustainable and equitable world.

4

The Trailblazers

The eco-entrepreneurial movement is a tapestry of diverse individuals, each weaving their unique story into the larger narrative of sustainability and positive impact. In this chapter, we explore the lives and achievements of some of the most influential eco-entrepreneurs who have blazed a trail toward a greener, more sustainable future.

1. Wangari Maathai: The Tree Mother of Kenya

Wangari Maathai, a Kenyan environmentalist and political activist, left an indelible mark on the world through her work in reforestation and women's empowerment. She founded the Green Belt Movement, an organization focused on tree planting and environmental conservation. By engaging local women in tree-planting activities, Maathai not only restored the environment but also empowered communities and promoted sustainable livelihoods. Her work earned her the Nobel Peace Prize in 2004, making her the first African woman to receive the award.

2. Richard Branson: The Eco-Entrepreneur Maverick

Richard Branson, the founder of the Virgin Group, is renowned for his unconventional approach to business and his commitment to environmental sustainability. He has championed green initiatives in various sectors, including transportation and energy. Virgin Galactic, his space tourism venture, seeks to make space travel more environmentally friendly. Branson's commitment to sustainability has influenced the airline and travel industry and inspired other entrepreneurs to pursue environmentally responsible business practices.

3. Wang Shu: Architect of Sustainable Dreams

Wang Shu, a Chinese architect, has gained international recognition for his work that combines traditional Chinese architectural techniques with modern sustainable design principles. He founded the Amateur Architecture Studio, which focuses on preserving cultural heritage and promoting eco-friendly construction methods. Wang's innovative designs, which incorporate locally-sourced materials and emphasize energy efficiency, have redefined architectural norms and highlighted the importance of preserving cultural heritage while embracing sustainability.

4. Janine Benyus: Biomimicry's Visionary

Janine Benyus is a biologist, innovation consultant, and author known for her work in biomimicry, a design principle that draws inspiration from nature's processes and structures. Benyus has influenced a new wave of eco-entrepreneurs by promoting the idea that solutions to environmental challenges can be found in the natural world. Her Biomimicry Institute and Biomimicry 3.8 consultancy have assisted businesses in creating sustainable, nature-inspired innovations.

5. N.R. Narayana Murthy: The IT Eco-Pioneer

N.R. Narayana Murthy, the co-founder of Infosys, is a key figure in India's information technology revolution. Beyond his contributions to the tech industry, he has been a proponent of responsible business practices and environmental sustainability. Murthy initiated several environmental and social initiatives within Infosys, including energy efficiency measures, waste reduction, and social responsibility programs. His approach has influenced the IT industry's approach to corporate social responsibility and sustainability in India.

6. Lisa Jackson: The Apple of Sustainable Innovation

Lisa Jackson, the former Environmental Protection Agency (EPA) administrator under the Obama administration, has played a pivotal role in pushing for corporate environmental responsibility. Her role as Apple's Vice President of Environment, Policy, and Social Initiatives exemplifies her commitment to integrating sustainability into business operations. Under her leadership, Apple has made substantial progress in reducing its environmental footprint and increasing the use of renewable energy in its supply chain.

These trailblazers have left an indelible mark on the eco-entrepreneurial movement, influencing industries, governments, and individuals to embrace sustainability as a guiding principle in their endeavors. Each has demonstrated that eco-consciousness and profitability can coexist, and their stories serve as powerful inspiration for the next generation of eco-entrepreneurs seeking to make a positive impact on the world while building successful businesses.

In the following chapters, we will explore the eco-entrepreneurial landscape in various sectors and regions, showcasing the remarkable individuals who have harnessed their entrepreneurial spirit to drive positive change and build a more sustainable and equitable world.

5

Sectoral Spotlight: Green Innovation Across Industries

Eco-entrepreneurship is not limited to one industry or region. It's a dynamic and versatile movement that has made an impact across a wide range of sectors. In this chapter, we'll shine a spotlight on eco-entrepreneurs who have made waves in various industries, demonstrating how green innovation can transform traditional businesses.

1. Energy and Cleantech: Elon Musk

Elon Musk, the CEO of Tesla and SpaceX, is a leading figure in the cleantech sector. He recognized the need to transition the world away from fossil fuels and pioneered the electric vehicle revolution. Tesla's electric cars and energy products have revolutionized the automotive and energy sectors, proving that sustainable solutions can be both practical and profitable.

2. Food and Agriculture: Kimbal Musk

Kimbal Musk, brother of Elon Musk, is a notable eco-entrepreneur in the food and agriculture industry. He co-founded The Kitchen, a family of restaurants that focuses on serving locally sourced, sustainably grown food. Musk's efforts in urban farming and community building have highlighted the importance of sustainable, locally produced food in reducing the environmental impact of our food systems.

3. Fashion: Stella McCartney

Stella McCartney, a British fashion designer, is renowned for her sustainable approach to the fashion industry. She founded her eponymous brand with a commitment to cruelty-free and environmentally responsible practices. McCartney's brand has proven that sustainability and luxury fashion can coexist, influencing the entire fashion industry to adopt more ethical and eco-conscious practices.

4. Technology: Jack Ma

Jack Ma, the co-founder of Alibaba Group, has been a driving force in sustainable e-commerce. Alibaba's Green Logistics initiative focuses on reducing the carbon footprint of the company's operations. Ma's commitment to environmental sustainability has led to significant progress in reducing waste and emissions in the e-commerce and technology sector.

5. Architecture and Construction: William McDonough

William McDonough is a pioneer in sustainable architecture and design. His innovative work includes the Cradle to Cradle design framework, which promotes products and buildings that are not only eco-friendly but also regenerative. McDonough's projects, such as the Green Building Council headquarters, demonstrate the potential of sustainable architecture to create beautiful, functional, and environmentally responsible structures.

6. Tourism and Hospitality: Costas Christ

Costas Christ, a global expert in sustainable tourism, has played a significant role in transforming the tourism and hospitality industry. As a consultant and advocate for responsible travel, he has worked with hotels, resorts, and governments to implement eco-friendly practices that benefit local communities and ecosystems. His efforts have raised awareness about the impact of tourism on the environment and the importance of responsible travel.

These eco-entrepreneurs represent a small fraction of the innovators who have pushed the boundaries of sustainability within their respective industries. Their achievements underscore the idea that green innovation is not confined to a single sector but can be applied across a wide range of industries. The success of these individuals serves as a testament to the broader potential for businesses to embrace eco-conscious practices and drive meaningful change in their fields.

In the upcoming chapters, we will delve deeper into the stories of eco-entrepreneurs who have achieved remarkable success in their specific sectors and have paved the way for a more sustainable and responsible future in business.

6

Regional Resonance: Eco-Entrepreneurship Around the World

Eco-entrepreneurship is a global phenomenon, with entrepreneurs from diverse regions contributing to the green business revolution. In this chapter, we'll explore the regional resonance of eco-entrepreneurship, highlighting some of the inspiring figures who have made significant contributions in their respective parts of the world.

1. Europe: Sir Richard Branson

Sir Richard Branson, a British entrepreneur, has been a trailblazer in the European eco-entrepreneurship scene. His diverse business ventures, from Virgin Atlantic to Virgin Galactic, have consistently emphasized environmental sustainability. Branson's influence extends beyond business, as he has actively supported efforts to combat climate change and promote renewable energy across Europe.

2. North America: Elon Musk

Elon Musk, a South African-born entrepreneur who later became an American citizen, is a prominent figure in North American eco-entrepreneurship. His groundbreaking work with Tesla, SpaceX, and SolarCity has reshaped the energy and transportation sectors. Musk's vision for sustainable innovation has had a profound impact in the United States and beyond.

3. Asia: Jack Ma

Jack Ma, the co-founder of Alibaba Group, has been a driving force for eco-entrepreneurship in Asia. His efforts in sustainable e-commerce and logistics have set a precedent for responsible business practices in the region. Ma's influence on green innovation extends to his home country, China, and serves as a model for businesses seeking to adopt eco-friendly practices.

4. South America: Felipe Villela

Felipe Villela, a Brazilian entrepreneur, is making waves in South America's eco-entrepreneurship landscape. He co-founded reNature, an organization dedicated to regenerative agriculture and sustainable farming practices. Villela's work focuses on the regeneration of degraded ecosystems and the promotion of responsible land management in South American agriculture.

5. Africa: Sam Kodo

Sam Kodo, a Togolese entrepreneur, is pioneering sustainable technology in Africa. He co-founded AgroCenta, a platform that connects smallholder farmers with markets and financial services. Kodo's efforts are contributing to food security and economic empowerment in rural Africa while promoting eco-friendly agriculture practices.

6. Oceania: David Trubridge

David Trubridge, a New Zealand-based eco-entrepreneur, has made a significant impact in Oceania with his sustainable design principles. He is known for his environmentally responsible lighting and furniture designs that incorporate natural materials and are inspired by nature. Trubridge's work reflects the connection between design, nature, and sustainability, resonating with the eco-conscious culture of the region.

These regional eco-entrepreneurs have not only shaped the sustainable business landscape in their respective parts of the world but have also contributed to the global green business movement. Their commitment to sustainability, innovation, and responsible business practices transcends geographical boundaries, serving as an inspiration for eco-entrepreneurs worldwide.

In the upcoming chapters, we will delve into more stories of eco-entrepreneurs across regions, shedding light on their unique contributions to the global movement of building a more sustainable and responsible business world.

7

Nurturing Sustainable Ecosystems

Eco-entrepreneurs understand that their businesses do not exist in isolation; they are part of larger ecosystems that include suppliers, consumers, communities, and the environment. In this chapter, we will explore the importance of nurturing these sustainable ecosystems and how eco-entrepreneurs have championed the cause.

1. Supply Chain Sustainability

Eco-entrepreneurs recognize the significance of a sustainable supply chain. They work closely with suppliers to ensure responsible sourcing, ethical practices, and reduced environmental impact. For example, Patagonia, under the leadership of Yvon Chouinard, has implemented strict environmental and social standards within its supply chain, promoting fair labor practices and minimizing the environmental footprint of its products.

2. Circular Economy

Many eco-entrepreneurs are proponents of the circular economy, where products and materials are reused, remanufactured, or recycled to reduce waste and conserve resources. Companies like Interface, led by Ray Anderson, have embraced this concept, redesigning their manufacturing processes and products to minimize waste and foster sustainability.

3. Local and Community Engagement

Eco-entrepreneurs often engage with local communities to create positive social and environmental impacts. They understand that businesses can be a force for good by supporting community development. For instance, Kimbal Musk's restaurant concept, The Kitchen, collaborates with local farmers and invests in urban farming initiatives, strengthening local economies and promoting sustainable agriculture.

4. Eco-Conscious Consumer Engagement

Eco-entrepreneurs prioritize building a customer base that values sustainability. They educate and engage their customers on eco-friendly practices and encourage them to make environmentally responsible choices. The Body Shop, founded by Anita Roddick, has not only produced ethical and eco-conscious products but has also actively involved its customers in campaigns for social and environmental causes.

5. Government and Policy Advocacy

Many eco-entrepreneurs advocate for environmentally friendly policies and regulations. They recognize the need for a supportive legislative environment that encourages sustainable practices. These entrepreneurs, such as Lisa Jackson of Apple, actively engage with governments and organizations to promote and shape policies that benefit the environment.

6. Collaborative Innovation

Eco-entrepreneurs often collaborate with other businesses, nonprofits, and organizations to foster innovation and address global sustainability challenges. The B Corp Movement, co-founded by Jay Coen Gilbert, Bart Houlahan, and Andrew Kassoy, exemplifies how businesses can work together to drive systemic change and collectively address environmental and social issues.

The success of eco-entrepreneurs in nurturing sustainable ecosystems illustrates that businesses can be both profitable and responsible. By considering the broader impacts of their operations, these entrepreneurs create a ripple effect of positive change that extends far beyond their own organizations. Their holistic approach to sustainability sets an example for businesses of all sizes and industries to follow.

In the following chapters, we will delve deeper into the stories of eco-entrepreneurs who have excelled in building and nurturing sustainable ecosystems, showcasing their strategies and successes in promoting responsible business practices.

8

Challenges and Resilience

The journey of eco-entrepreneurship is not without its challenges. In this chapter, we'll explore the obstacles and setbacks that eco-entrepreneurs often face, as well as the resilience they exhibit in overcoming these hurdles.

1. Financial Challenges

Eco-entrepreneurs may encounter financial challenges, including the high upfront costs of sustainable practices, difficulties in securing funding, or navigating markets where eco-friendly products and services are still gaining acceptance. Overcoming these financial hurdles requires innovative financing strategies and a long-term vision.

2. Regulatory and Policy Roadblocks

Government regulations and policies can either support or hinder eco-entrepreneurship. Bureaucratic obstacles and inconsistent policies can create uncertainty and increase costs for eco-friendly businesses. Successful eco-entrepreneurs often engage in advocacy and work with policymakers to influence change.

3. Market Competition

Competing in markets dominated by conventional, non-sustainable products can be challenging. Eco-entrepreneurs may face resistance from consumers who are accustomed to traditional options or are unwilling to pay a premium for eco-friendly alternatives. It requires effective marketing and education to win over customers.

4. Scaling Sustainable Practices

Expanding eco-friendly practices across a growing business can be complex. As a business grows, maintaining sustainability can become more challenging, but it's essential for eco-entrepreneurs to preserve their core values while scaling operations.

5. Supply Chain Sustainability

Ensuring a sustainable supply chain can be difficult, especially when working with suppliers who may not share the same eco-conscious values. Collaborating with suppliers to meet sustainability standards while maintaining product quality and cost-effectiveness is an ongoing challenge for eco-entrepreneurs.

6. Balancing Profit and Purpose

Balancing profitability with a commitment to environmental and social responsibility can be a delicate act. Eco-entrepreneurs must continually navigate this tension, demonstrating that it is possible to achieve both goals.

7. Resilience and Innovation

Eco-entrepreneurs are characterized by their resilience in the face of adversity. They view challenges as opportunities for innovation and growth. These entrepreneurs adapt to changing circumstances and continue to drive their businesses forward with a deep commitment to their environmental and social missions.

8. Collaborative Solutions

To overcome challenges, many eco-entrepreneurs turn to collaboration and partnerships. By working with like-minded organizations and sharing knowledge, they can find solutions that may be difficult to achieve independently.

9. Continuous Learning

Eco-entrepreneurs understand that the journey toward sustainability is an ongoing process. They stay informed about the latest developments in eco-friendly technology, market trends, and sustainability practices. This commitment to continuous learning allows them to adapt and remain at the forefront of their industries.

In the following chapters, we will explore in greater detail how eco-entrepreneurs have confronted and surmounted these challenges in their pursuit of a more sustainable and responsible business world. Their stories of resilience and determination serve as a testament to the power of eco-entrepreneurship in creating positive change.

9

Sustainable Success Stories

In this chapter, we delve into a collection of inspiring success stories from the world of eco-entrepreneurship. These stories showcase the incredible achievements of entrepreneurs who have not only built profitable businesses but have also made a significant positive impact on the environment and society.

1. Elon Musk and the Electric Revolution

Elon Musk's visionary approach to sustainable transportation has transformed the automotive industry. Through Tesla, he has made electric vehicles mainstream, challenging the dominance of gasoline-powered cars and accelerating the transition to sustainable energy sources. Musk's success is not only measured in profits but also in his pioneering work to combat climate change.

2. Patagonia: Profitable Activism

Patagonia, founded by Yvon Chouinard, has blended environmental advocacy with commerce. The company's commitment to eco-friendly products and ethical business practices has resonated with consumers, creating a loyal customer base and robust sales. Patagonia's activism, including its "Don't Buy This Jacket" campaign, has highlighted the importance of responsible consumption.

3. Interface: From Wasteful to Waste-Free

Ray Anderson, the late founder of Interface, transformed his carpet manufacturing company into an environmental leader. He set the goal of becoming a "restorative enterprise" with zero environmental footprint. By adopting sustainable practices, redesigning products, and committing to a circular economy, Interface has made remarkable progress toward this goal.

4. The Body Shop: Ethical Beauty

Anita Roddick, the founder of The Body Shop, built an ethical beauty brand that challenged the cosmetics industry. The company's commitment to cruelty-free products and environmentally responsible practices demonstrated that beauty and ethics could coexist. Roddick's legacy lives on through The Body Shop's continued dedication to ethical standards.

5. SolarCity and Lyndon Rive

Lyndon Rive co-founded SolarCity to make solar energy more accessible. The company revolutionized the solar industry by providing affordable solar solutions for homeowners and businesses. SolarCity's innovative business model and commitment to clean energy contributed to the growth of the solar power sector.

6. Grameen Bank: Microfinance for Empowerment

Muhammad Yunus, the founder of Grameen Bank, pioneered the concept of microfinance to empower the poor and promote sustainable economic development. His innovative approach has not only transformed the financial industry but has also uplifted millions of people out of poverty.

These success stories illustrate that eco-entrepreneurship is not a mere ideal but a practical and profitable approach to business. Eco-entrepreneurs have shown that companies can thrive while making a positive impact on the environment and society. These stories serve as powerful examples for aspiring eco-entrepreneurs, demonstrating that sustainability and profitability can go hand in hand.

In the next chapter, we will explore the broader implications of eco-entrepreneurship for the future of business, the environment, and society as a whole.

10

The Future of Eco-Entrepreneurship

Eco-entrepreneurship is not just a passing trend; it's a movement that continues to gain momentum and reshape the business landscape. In this final chapter, we'll look at the future of eco-entrepreneurship and its broader implications for the environment, society, and the business world.

1. The Sustainability Imperative

As the world grapples with urgent environmental challenges, sustainability has become an imperative. Eco-entrepreneurs are at the forefront of this movement, driving change and offering practical solutions to address climate change, resource depletion, and ecological degradation. The future of business will be increasingly defined by eco-conscious practices.

2. Mainstream Adoption

Eco-friendly products and services are moving from niche markets to mainstream adoption. More consumers are choosing sustainable options, and businesses are responding by incorporating environmental responsibility into their operations. The eco-entrepreneurship model will continue to shape consumer preferences and drive sustainable innovation in various industries.

3. Regulatory and Policy Support

Governments and regulatory bodies are recognizing the importance of sustainable practices. They are implementing policies and incentives to support green initiatives. Eco-entrepreneurs will benefit from this evolving policy landscape, which may include tax incentives, grants, and regulations that promote sustainability.

4. Collaborative Initiatives

Eco-entrepreneurs will increasingly engage in collaborative initiatives that transcend industry boundaries. Partnerships between businesses, non-profits, and governments will drive systemic change, leading to more holistic and effective solutions to environmental and social challenges.

5. Advancements in Green Technology

The rapid advancement of green technology, from renewable energy solutions to sustainable materials and circular economy innovations, will provide eco-entrepreneurs with more tools to create environmentally responsible products and services. These technological advancements will drive economic growth and sustainability.

6. A Cultural Shift

Eco-entrepreneurship has sparked a cultural shift towards more responsible and conscious consumer behavior. People are becoming more aware of the impact of their choices and are seeking products and services that align with their values. This shift in culture will continue to influence markets and businesses.

7. The Power of the Consumer

Consumers have the power to drive change. Their choices and demands for eco-friendly products and ethical business practices are influencing the decisions of businesses. The future of eco-entrepreneurship is closely tied to consumer expectations and preferences.

8. Global Collaboration for Climate Action

Eco-entrepreneurs will play a crucial role in global climate action efforts. They will work together to reduce greenhouse gas emissions, promote sustainable practices, and contribute to international efforts to combat climate change.

9. The Next Generation of Eco-Entrepreneurs

The future will see a new generation of eco-entrepreneurs emerging, bringing fresh ideas and perspectives to the sustainability movement. They will build on the foundations laid by their predecessors and continue to drive the green business revolution forward.

10. A Blueprint for Responsible Business

Eco-entrepreneurship serves as a blueprint for responsible business in the 21st century. The values and practices of eco-entrepreneurs will become integral to the way businesses operate, creating a more sustainable, equitable, and environmentally conscious global economy.

Eco-entrepreneurship is not just a business strategy; it's a way of reimagining the relationship between commerce and the environment. It offers a path to prosperity that harmonizes with the health of the planet and the well-being of people. As we move into the future, the influence of eco-entrepreneurs will continue to expand, shaping a world where sustainability and success go hand in hand.

11

Taking Action: Becoming an Eco-Entrepreneur

In this chapter, we'll explore the steps and strategies for those who aspire to become eco-entrepreneurs. If you're inspired by the stories and principles of eco-entrepreneurship and wish to embark on your own journey toward building a sustainable and responsible business, this chapter is your guide.

1. Identify Your Passion and Purpose

Start by identifying your passion and the environmental or social issues you're most passionate about. Your business should align with your values and mission, as this passion will drive your commitment and resilience.

2. Conduct a Sustainability Audit

Examine your business concept and processes to assess their environmental and social impact. Identify areas where you can incorporate eco-friendly practices and principles. Consider factors like energy efficiency, waste reduction, and sustainable sourcing.

3. Set Clear Sustainability Goals

Establish concrete sustainability goals for your business. Whether it's reducing carbon emissions, promoting ethical labor practices, or minimizing waste, having clear objectives will guide your efforts and help you measure progress.

4. Innovate and Differentiate

Innovation is at the core of eco-entrepreneurship. Look for unique and environmentally responsible solutions to address your market's needs. Differentiate your business by offering products or services that stand out in terms of sustainability and quality.

5. Collaborate and Network

Build relationships with like-minded entrepreneurs, nonprofits, and organizations. Collaborative efforts can lead to shared resources, knowledge, and opportunities for positive impact. Networking within the eco-entrepreneurship community can provide support and inspiration.

6. Embrace Sustainable Marketing

Communicate your sustainability efforts and values to your target audience. Use eco-friendly packaging, promote ethical sourcing, and highlight your commitment to the environment. Transparency and authenticity are key to winning the trust of eco-conscious consumers.

7. Seek Funding and Resources

Explore eco-friendly financing options, such as impact investing, grants, and eco-focused crowdfunding platforms. Consider accelerators and incubators dedicated to sustainability and green innovation.

8. Engage with the Community

Become an active part of your local and global communities. Participate in environmental events, support local causes, and engage with stakeholders to promote eco-conscious practices and community development.

9. Adapt and Iterate

The journey of an eco-entrepreneur is marked by adaptation and continuous learning. Be open to feedback and willing to adjust your business practices based on the lessons you learn along the way.

10. Measure and Report Impact

Quantify the environmental and social impact of your business. Regularly measure and report your progress toward sustainability goals. Use these metrics to track your success and share your achievements with stakeholders.

11. Stay Committed to Your Mission

Eco-entrepreneurship is a long-term commitment. There will be challenges and setbacks, but your dedication to your mission will drive your resilience and innovation.

12. Inspire Others

Lead by example and inspire others to join the eco-entrepreneurship movement. Share your journey, knowledge, and success stories to encourage more individuals and businesses to embrace sustainable practices.

As you embark on your eco-entrepreneurial journey, remember that it's not just about building a business; it's about creating a better, more sustainable world. Your efforts, passion, and commitment can drive positive change in the business landscape, contributing to a greener, more equitable future.

12

A Call to Action

Eco-entrepreneurship is not limited to a select group of individuals. It's a call to action for everyone who recognizes the urgent need to address environmental and social challenges while building a sustainable future. In this chapter, we issue a call to action to individuals, businesses, and society as a whole.

1. Individuals: Be Informed and Engaged

- Educate yourself about environmental and social issues, and understand how your daily choices impact these challenges.
    - Support eco-friendly businesses and products by making informed consumer decisions.
    - Advocate for sustainability in your workplace, community, and government.
    - Consider becoming an eco-entrepreneur yourself, whether by starting a green business or supporting one.

2. Businesses: Integrate Sustainability

- Embrace eco-entrepreneurship by incorporating sustainability into your business model.
- Set clear sustainability goals and regularly measure and report your environmental and social impact.
- Innovate to reduce waste, minimize emissions, and use resources more efficiently.
- Collaborate with other businesses, nonprofits, and government organizations to drive systemic change.

3. Governments and Policymakers: Foster a Sustainable Ecosystem

- Implement regulations and incentives that promote sustainable business practices.
- Support research and development in green technology and innovation.
- Partner with businesses and organizations to address pressing environmental and social challenges.
- Prioritize sustainability and environmental protection in public policy.

4. Educators: Cultivate Eco-Entrepreneurial Mindsets

- Integrate sustainability and eco-entrepreneurship into educational curricula.
- Inspire the next generation to consider eco-friendly practices in their career choices.
- Create opportunities for students to engage in real-world eco-entrepreneurship projects.

5. Nonprofits and Organizations: Amplify Impact

- Support and promote eco-entrepreneurship initiatives that align with your mission.
- Collaborate with businesses to drive positive social and environmental change.
- Advocate for sustainability and responsible practices in your field.

6. Investors and Funders: Support Green Innovation

- Invest in eco-entrepreneurial ventures and green startups.
    - Prioritize businesses that are dedicated to environmental and social responsibility.
    - Provide funding and mentorship to entrepreneurs who are committed to sustainability.

7. Media and Communication: Amplify Eco-Entrepreneurial Stories

- Use your platform to highlight the achievements of eco-entrepreneurs.
    - Raise awareness about environmental and social issues and the impact of sustainable business practices.
    - Encourage consumer and business engagement in eco-friendly endeavors.

8. Communities: Support Local Eco-Entrepreneurs

- Embrace and celebrate eco-entrepreneurs within your community.
    - Patronize eco-friendly businesses and encourage others to do the same.
    - Foster a culture of sustainability, where businesses, residents, and local governments collaborate for a greener future.

9. Scientists and Innovators: Pioneer Sustainable Solutions

- Innovate and develop new technologies and practices that address environmental challenges.
    - Collaborate with eco-entrepreneurs to bring these solutions to the market.
    - Champion the integration of scientific research into practical eco-entrepreneurial endeavors.

10. Global Collaboration: Unite for a Sustainable World

- Recognize that environmental and social challenges are global, and solutions require international cooperation.

- Engage in cross-border partnerships and initiatives that address climate change, resource conservation, and social equity on a global scale.

Eco-entrepreneurship is not a solitary endeavor; it's a collective mission to build a better, more sustainable world. Each individual, business, organization, and government has a vital role to play. By answering the call to action and embracing eco-entrepreneurial principles, we can work together to create a future where prosperity, sustainability, and social responsibility are intertwined, fostering a world that is greener, more equitable, and better for all.

In this comprehensive book, "Eco-Entrepreneurs: Building a Green Business Revolution," we embark on a journey through the world of eco-entrepreneurship. We explore the stories, strategies, and impact of eco-entrepreneurs who have embraced sustainability, environmental responsibility, and social consciousness as core principles in their business endeavors.

Each chapter delves into a specific aspect of eco-entrepreneurship, from the inspiring stories of influential eco-entrepreneurs like Elon Musk, Richard Branson, and Anita Roddick, to the sectoral spotlight on green innovation across various industries, including energy, food, fashion, and technology. We also examine the regional resonance of eco-entrepreneurship across Europe, North America, Asia, and other regions.

The book emphasizes the importance of nurturing sustainable ecosystems, promoting ethical supply chains, and fostering circular economies. It discusses the challenges faced by eco-entrepreneurs and the resilience they exhibit in overcoming obstacles. The stories of success highlight the achievements of eco-entrepreneurs who have built profitable businesses while making a significant positive impact on the environment and society.

The book looks toward the future of eco-entrepreneurship, emphasizing the sustainability imperative, mainstream adoption, regulatory and policy support, collaborative initiatives, advancements in green technology, a cultural shift, and the rise of the next generation of eco-entrepreneurs. It calls on individuals, businesses, governments, educators, nonprofits, investors, and media to answer the call to action, fostering a world where prosperity, sustainability, and social responsibility are intertwined.

In the end, "Eco-Entrepreneurs" serves as a guide for those who wish to become eco-entrepreneurs, illustrating the steps and strategies needed to build a sustainable and responsible business. It showcases the power of eco-entrepreneurship in addressing environmental and social challenges and creating a more sustainable and equitable world.

www.ingramcontent.com/pod-product-compliance
Lightning Source LLC
LaVergne TN
LVHW020455080526
838202LV00057B/5962